REAL
mvpkids®

I Can Brush My Teeth™

Sophia Day®

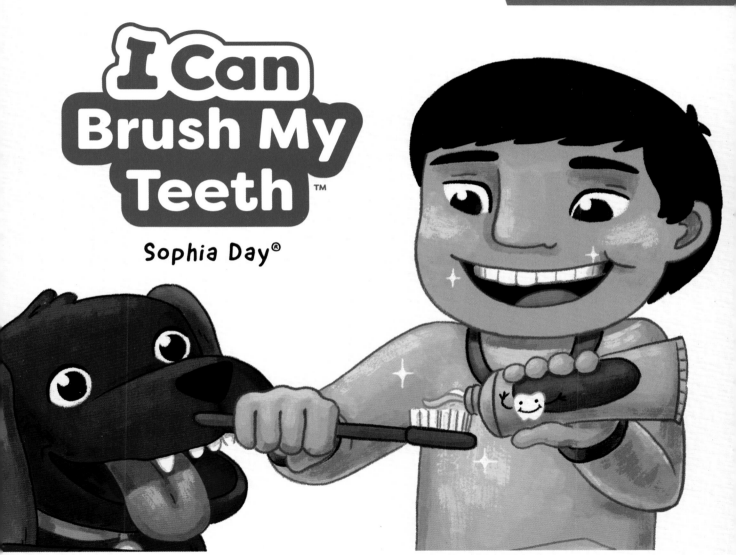

Written by Celestte Dills   *Illustrated by* Timothy Zowada

The Sophia Day® Creative Team-

Celestte Dills, Timothy Zowada, Stephanie Strouse, Megan Johnson, Kayla Pearson, Patty Lopez Gregersen, Vanessa Moore, Mel Sauder

A **special thank you** to our reviewers who graciously give us feedback, edits, and help ensure that our products remain accurate, applicable, and genuinely diverse.

Published and Distributed by MVP Kids Media, LLC - Mesa, Arizona, USA

Designed by Stephanie Strouse

ISBN 9781637959312
DOM Feb 2022
Job # 17-003-01

May your childhood be filled with adventure, your days with hope and your learnings with wisdom, and may you continuously grow as an MVP Kid, preparing to lead a responsible, meaningful life.

– Sophia Day

Hello! I'm Yong . . .

and this is my pet dog, Luna.

I help Luna be healthy by
giving her food and water . . .

taking her for walks,

brushing her fur . . .

4

. . . and even brushing her teeth.

I can brush my teeth to
be healthy and take care of myself.

When I was younger, I didn't know
how or when to brush my teeth.

I put toothpaste on my toothbrush.

I brush my teeth for two minutes:

back to front . . .

top to bottom.

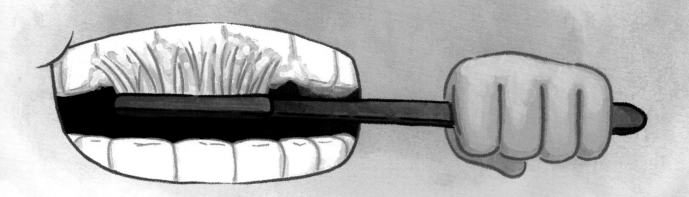

I carefully spit
toothpaste into the sink.

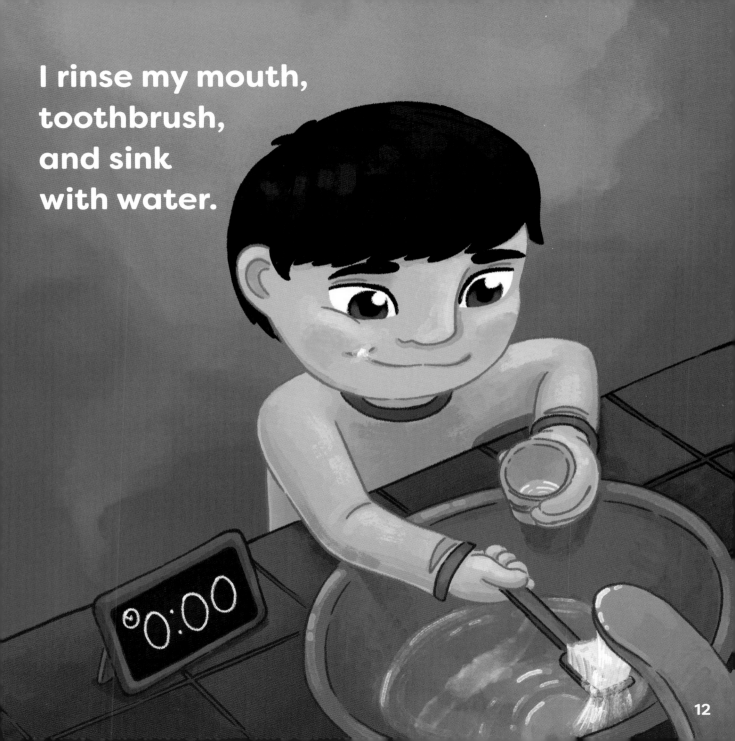

I rinse my mouth,
toothbrush,
and sink
with water.

When I get ready
to start my day . . .

I can brush my teeth.

When I eat a sweet treat . . .

I can brush my teeth.

When I am getting ready for bed . . .

I brush my
teeth . . .

to make them clean and to help me be healthy.

20

TOOTHBRUSHING STEPS

1. Put my toothpaste on my toothbrush.

2. Brush my teeth: front, back . . .

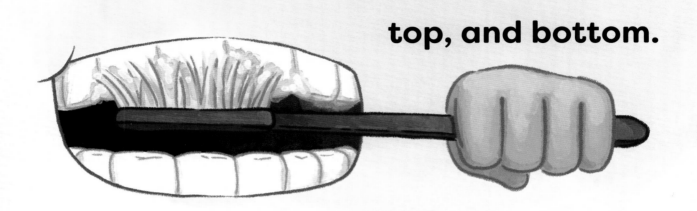

top, and bottom.

3. Rinse my mouth, toothbrush, and sink.

meet our
mvpkids®

featured in
I Can Brush My Teeth™

Hi! My name is Yong Chen.

I want to be a chef when I grow up. I love to watch my mom and grandfather cook. My dad travels a lot for his job, but when he is home, I love to do special things with him. After I brush my teeth at night, I read my favorite MVP Kids' books before falling asleep.

Also featuring . . .

Mr. Huang Chen
Father

Mrs. Li Chen
Mother

Lily Chen
Sister

Luna
Pet Dog

HELPFUL TEACHING TIPS
I Can Brush My Teeth

According to the Centers for Disease Control and Prevention, while preventable, cavities are one of the most common childhood chronic diseases. You can help your child prevent cavities by:
- brushing twice and flossing once each day
- eating a healthy diet low in sugar and processed foods
- seeing a dentist for regular check-ups

Toothbrushing Steps

The steps for brushing teeth are:

1. Put toothpaste* on my toothbrush**.
2. Brush my teeth: front, back, top, and bottom.
3. Rinse my mouth, toothbrush, and sink.

Make a copy of the steps on pages 21-22 and display it in the bathroom at children's eye level.

*If your child is under two, consult your dentist before using toothpaste.
**If your child does not have teeth yet, consult your dentist before using a toothbrush.

Brush, Brush, Brush

Teach your child to use a small amount of toothpaste, about the size of a pea. Remind your child to spit toothpaste into the sink if it becomes too foamy, when finished brushing, and after rinsing with water.

Help your child use circular motions to gently brush from back to front and top to bottom. Remind your child to brush all surfaces: teeth, gums, tongue, and roof of mouth.

It is recommended to brush teeth for approximately two minutes. That's enough time to hum the ABC Song three times. Consider humming while brushing your teeth or set a timer for two minutes.

I Can:

- **put my toothpaste on my toothbrush;**
- **brush my teeth front, back, top, and bottom;**
- **rinse my mouth and toothbrush.**

Fun with Brushing Teeth

Try this activity to help your child practice brushing and flossing. **You will need:**

- A white ice cube tray
- A dry erase marker (with adult supervision)
- An unused toothbrush
- Water
- Modeling clay
- A piece of yarn about six inches long

Instructions:

Turn the ice cube tray upside down in a place that can get wet and messy. Use the dry erase marker to color on the cups. Dip the toothbrush in water and use it to brush away the marker. Press the modeling clay into the spaces between the ice cube tray cups. Use the yarn to floss away the clay.

Eating Healthy

Healthy teeth begin with eating healthy foods. Help your child identify healthy foods with this activity. **You will need:**

- Paper
- Writing utensil
- Pictures of foods that are healthy and not healthy (cut from magazines or printed)
- Glue

Instructions:

Draw a simple outline of a tooth on the paper. Encourage your child to identify which foods are healthy and glue the healthy foods onto the tooth.

CELEBRATE! Series

Board Books Ages 2-5

Paperbacks Ages 4-8

MIGHTY TOKENS Read Together

Ages 4-8

Playful Apprentice
Real Work Real Play
Ages 4-10

---

help me become
Ages 4-10

---

help me understand
Ages 6-12

I Can Be an MVP!™
Ages 2-6

SOPHIA DAY'S®
instill® SEL
Instill Character®
FOR THE CLASSROOM

SOPHIA DAY'S®
instill® SEL
AT HOME

Our Instill® SEL programs are available in English and Spanish with bilingual tools!

Instill character® and strengthen mental health strategies in the classroom or at home with our social and emotional learning (SEL) programs for early learners!

Our classroom curriculum and home programs give you tools and strategies to develop your students' and family's healthy social and emotional skills and behaviors.

Learn more at MVPKids.com.

Yong Chen

Leo Russo

Frankie Russo

Julia Rojas

Aanya Patel

Annie James

Blake James

Sarah Cohen-Goldstein